12-20-97

MW00622590

AGGRESSIVE
Christianity

AGGRESSIVE
Christianity

CATHERINE BOOTH

Edited with an Introduction by
Lyle W. Dorsett

Aggressive Christianity
by Catherine Booth
Edited with an Introduction by Lyle W. Dorsett
Used by permission

Published by World Wide Publications 1993
in cooperation with the Institute of Evangelism,
Billy Graham Center, Wheaton, IL

ISBN: 0-89066-238-X
Printed in the United States of America

Contents

Introduction

Chapter 1
Aggressive Christianity
13

Chapter 2
The World's Need
33

Introduction

Raised in a strict English Methodist home where she was encouraged to read the Bible and study Wesleyan hymns daily, Catherine (Kate) Mumford attended worship services regularly and poured considerable energy into the British Christian Temperance movement. All of her religious activity notwithstanding, she had neither inner peace nor assurance of salvation.

In 1845, at age sixteen, Kate Mumford experienced a profound conversion. For some time, this very attractive young woman with slight build, lustrous dark hair, and strikingly beautiful brown eyes, went to bed with her Bible and hymnbook under the pillow. Her fervent prayer was that she might awaken in the morning with a genuine confidence in her salvation. Soon thereafter she woke up one morning, opened her hymnal and read these lines by Charles Wesley:

> My God, I am thine!
> What a comfort divine!
> What a blessing to know
> that my Jesus is mine!

Wesley's words pierced her heart. From that moment on, she was a new creature who gradually knew Jesus Christ better, loved Him more, and grew increasingly burdened to make Him known to others.

Six years later another event changed Kate's life. At a religious gathering in her home town in Derbyshire, she heard a strong sermon by a twenty-two-year-old preacher named William Booth. Later, the two of them met socially at a friend's home. Immediately the tall, pale-faced young man with jet black hair and fiery eyes fell mightily in love with the brilliant, outspoken, and vivacious Kate. She was powerfully drawn to this preacher who was her same age, and soon the two were betrothed and committed to a life of marriage and ministry.

The couple married in 1855, while William served as a traveling evangelist with the New Methodist Connection. In 1861, however, the Methodist leaders in annual conference stripped Booth of his freedom to itinerate as an evangelist. He was told to oversee local congregations and give up the work of evangelism.

When this order was announced from the floor an inflamed Catherine Booth cried, "Never," from the crowded gallery. The devoted wife and mother of four walked out of the conference. Within a few minutes William Booth followed his wife from the meeting hall. Together they vowed to leave the Methodist church and follow God's call to take the Gospel message to England's most impoverished and decadent urban masses.

At age thirty-two, Catherine and William Booth gave up salary and security. On their own, but with a keen sense of the Holy Spirit's guidance, they set out on a pilgrimage that led them into an ambitiously holistic urban ministry. They were determined to tell every drunk, drug addict, prostitute, vagrant, and orphan they could find that Jesus Christ had taken upon Himself the penalty for the sins of everyone who would call upon His name for mercy.

Catherine Booth, like her husband, believed that the earth was embroiled in a mighty spiritual war. Satan had a death grip on the urban poor, but Jesus Christ had come to destroy the work of the evil one. Consequently, Catherine and William set out to break down the gates of hell by telling the captives what Christ Jesus had done for them. Furthermore, they wanted to break the bondage of poverty, addiction, and hopelessness that gripped these helpless city dwellers.

Because of the urgency of the urban crisis, Catherine Booth became an aggressive ally of her husband. She began preaching alongside of William and the men who had joined them. She also invited other women to join the work. By 1878, they founded the Salvation Army. From its ranks, they preached the Good News of the Kingdom of God; and in Jesus Christ's name, they fed the hungry, clothed the poor, housed the widows and orphans, and helped rehabilitate and employ those who had previously been the flotsam and jetsam of society.

The co-founder of the Salvation Army and mother of eight children died in 1890 at the age of sixty-one. During nearly three decades of ministry, God used her to liberate thousands of women and men from the bondage of personal sin and the shackles of urban poverty through an evangelistic organization and holistic ministry that was spreading all over the world.

Catherine Booth also played a key role in establishing the right of women to preach. Furthermore, she helped combat the exploitation of women and children, and she demonstrated that disciples of Jesus Christ could meet the physical needs of people while simultaneously ministering to their lost and broken souls.

Catherine Booth and her husband left the Methodist church because they felt it had grown comfortable and complacent. Indeed, by 1861 many Methodist leaders seemed to be offended by evangelism and appeared to be calloused toward the poor. But Catherine Booth was convinced that she and her husband and all who would join them were commissioned by Christ to proclaim the Good News to the poor. The huddled masses, she believed, comprised a great harvest. What was lacking, however, was an aggressive work force to bundle and bring in the sheaves.

The two messages that follow were preached by Mrs. Booth, as she liked to be addressed, in London in 1880. She agreed to have them published three years later in hopes that indolent Christians would be aroused to go out aggressively into the highways and hedges and compel the perishing masses to come into the Great Feast that God had prepared for them.

These two sermons were originally printed in a little volume of sermons entitled *Aggressive Christianity* (Philadelphia: National Publishing Company for the Promotion of Holiness, 1883). Both messages have been slightly abridged and edited.

For more information on the life and ministry of Catherine Booth see:

Mildred Duff, *Catherine Booth: A Sketch* (1914); F.De L. Booth Tucker, *The Life of Catherine Booth: The Mother of the Salvation Army (1892),* 2 vols.

Lyle W. Dorsett
Wheaton, Illinois, 1992

1

Aggressive Christianity

"Go ye into all the world, and preach the
Gospel to every creature."
—Mark 16:15

"And I said, Who art Thou, Lord?
And He said, I am Jesus whom thou
persecutest. But rise, and stand upon thy feet:
for I have appeared unto thee for this
purpose, to make thee a minister and a
witness both of these things which thou hast
seen, and of those things in the which I will
appear unto thee; delivering thee from the
people, and from the Gentiles, unto whom
now I send thee, to open their eyes, and
to turn the from darkness to light, and from
the power of Satan unto God, that
they may receive forgiveness of sins, and
inheritance among them which are
sanctified by faith that is in me."
—Acts 26:15–18

Suppose we could blot out from our minds
all knowledge of the history of Christianity
from the close of the period described as the

Acts of the Apostles; suppose we could detach from our minds all knowledge of the history of Christianity since then, and take the Acts of the Apostles and sit down and calculate what was likely to happen in the world, between then and now. We should have said, if we knew nothing of what has intervened from that time to this, that, no doubt, the world where that spiritual war commenced, would have long since been subjugated to the influence of the Originator and Founder! I say, from reading these Acts, and from observing the spirit which animated the early disciples, and from the way in which everything fell before them, we should have anticipated that ten thousand times greater results would have followed, and, in my judgment, this anticipation would have been perfectly rational and just.

We Christians profess to possess in the Gospel of Christ a mighty lever which, rightly and universally applied, would lift the entire burden of sin and misery from the souls of our fellowmen—a panacea, we believe it to be, for all the moral and spiritual woes of humanity, and in curing their spiritual plagues we should go far to cure their physical plagues also. We all profess to believe this. Christians have professed to believe this for generations gone by, ever since the time of which we have been reading, and yet, look at the world, look at so-called Christian England and America, in this end of the nineteenth century! The great majority of the nations utterly ignoring God, and not even making any pretence of remembering Him one day in a week.

And then, look at the rest of the world. I have frequently been so depressed with this view of things that I have felt as if my heart would break. I don't know how other Christians feel, but I can truly say that "rivers of water do often run down my eyes because men keep not His law" (see Psalm 119:136), and because it seems to me that this dispensation, com-pared with what God intended it to be, has been, and still is, as great a failure as that which preceded it.

Now, I ask, how is this? I do not for a moment believe that this is in accordance with the purpose of God. Some people have a very convenient way of hiding behind God's purposes, and saying, "Oh! He will do His own will." I wish He did! They say, "You know God's will is done after all." I wish it were! *He* says it is *not* done, and over and over again laments the fact. He wants it to be done, but it is NOT DONE! Again, they say, "It is of no use to stand up and propound theories that are at variance with things as they are." There has been a great deal too much of this, and it has had a very bad effect. The world is in this condition, and yet the Christian church was launched with such purposes, with such promises, and with such prospects, and yet nearly nineteen hundred years have rolled away and here we are. How little has been done, comparatively. What little change has been effected in the habits and dispositions of humankind.

But some of you will say, "Well, but there is a good deal done." Thank God for that. It would be sad if there were *nothing* done; but it looks like a drop in the ocean compared with what should have been done. Now I cannot accept any theory which so far reflects upon the love and goodness of God as to make *Him* to blame for this effeteness of Christianity. And, so far as my influence extends, I will not allow the responsibility and the blame of all this to be rolled back upon God, who so loved the world that He gave His only Son to ignominy and death in order to redeem the world. I do not believe it for a moment.

I believe that the old archenemy has done in this dispensation what he did in former ones—so far circumvented the purposes of God that he has succeeded in bringing about this state of things—in retarding the accomplishment of God's purposes and keeping the world thus largely under his own power and influence. I believe he has succeeded in doing this, as he has succeeded always before, by DECEIVING GOD'S OWN PEOPLE. He has always done so. He has always produced a caricature of God's real thing, and the nearer he can get it to be like the original the more successful his is. He has succeeded in deceiving God's people:

First, AS TO THE STANDARD OF THEIR OWN RELIGIOUS LIFE.

And, *second*, he has succeeded in deceiving them AS TO THEIR DUTIES AND OBLIGATIONS TO THE WORLD.

He has succeeded, first, in deceiving them as to the standard of their own religious life. He has led the church, nearly as a whole, to receive what I call an Oh-wretched-man-that-I-am religion! He has gotten them to lower the standard which Jesus Christ Himself established in this Book—a standard, not only to be aimed at, but to be attained unto—a standard of victory over sin, the world, the flesh, and the devil, *real, living, reigning, triumphing Christianity!* Satan knew what was the secret of the great success of those early disciples. It was their whole-hearted devotion, their absorbing love to Christ, their utter abnegation of the world. It was their entire absorption in the salvation of their fellow-men and the glory of their God. It was an enthusiastic religion that swallowed them up, and made them willing to become wanderers and vagabonds on the face of the earth—for His sake to dwell in dens and caves, to be torn asunder, and to be persecuted in every form.

It was this degree of devotion before which Satan saw he had no chance. Such people as these, he knew, must ultimately subdue the world. It is not in human nature to stand before that kind of spirit, that amount of love and zeal, and if Christians had only gone on as they began, the glorious prophecy would have been fulfilled. The kingdoms of this world would have become the kingdoms of our Lord and His Christ.

Therefore, the archenemy said, "What must I do? I shall be defeated after all. I shall lose my

supremacy as the god of this world. What shall
I do? No use to bring in a gigantic system of
error, which everybody will see to be error."
Oh, dear, no! That has never been Satan's way;
but his plan has been to get hold of a good man
here and there, who shall creep in, as the
Apostle said, unawares, and preach another
doctrine, and who shall deceive, if it were possible, the very elect. *And he did it.* He accom-
plished his design. He gradually lowered the
standard of Christian life and character, and
though, in every revival, God has raised it again
to a certain extent, we have never gotten com-
pletely back to the simplicity, purity, and devotion set before us in these Acts of the Apostles
and in the Epistles.

And just to the degree that it has approxi-
mated thereto, in every age, Satan has encouraged somebody to show that this was too high a
standard for human nature, altogether beyond
us, and that, therefore, Christians must sit
down and just be content to be Oh-wretched-
man-that-I-am people to the end of their days.
He has deceived the church into a condition
that makes one sometimes positively ashamed
to hear professing Christians talk; and
ashamed, also, that the world should hear them
talk. I do not wonder at thoughtful, intelligent
men being driven from such Christianity as
this. It would have driven me off, if I had not
known the *power* of godliness. I believe this
kind of Christianity has made more infidels
than all the infidel books ever written.

Yes, Satan knew that he must get Christians down from the high pinnacle of wholehearted consecration to God. He knew that he had no chance till he tempted them down from that blessed vantage ground. Therefore, he began to spread those false doctrines, to counteract what John wrote before he died. He saw what was coming, and sounded down the ages: "Little children, let no man deceive you: he that doeth righteousness is righteous, even as He is righteous. He that committeth sin is of the devil; for the devil sinneth from the beginning. For this purpose the Son of God was manifested, that he might destroy the works of the devil" (1 John 3:7–8). Lord, revive that doctrine! Help us afresh to put up the standard!

Oh, the great evil is that dishonest-hearted people, because they feel it condemns them, lower the standard to their miserable experience. I said, when I was young, and I repeat it in my maturer years, that if it sent me to hell I would never pull it down. Oh, that God's people felt like that. There is the glorious standard put before us. The power is proffered, the conditions laid down, and we CAN all attain it if we will; but if we will not—for the sake of the children, and for generations yet unborn—do not let us drag it down, and try to make it meet our little, paltry, circumscribed experience. LET US KEEP IT UP. This is the way to get the world to look at it. Show the world a real, living, self-sacrificing, hardworking, toiling, triumphing religion, and the world will be influenced by it; but anything short of that, they will turn around and spit upon!

Second, Satan has deceived even those whom he could not succeed in getting to lower the standard of their own lives with respect to their duties and obligations to the world.

I have been reading, of late, the New Testament with special reference to the aggressive spirit of Primitive Christianity, and it is wonderful what floods of light come upon you when you read the Bible with reference to any particular topic on which you are seeking help. When God sees you are panting after the light, in order that you may use it, *He pours it in upon you.* It is an indispensable condition of receiving light that you are willing to follow it. People say they don't see this and that; no, because they do not wish to see. They are not willing to walk in it, and, therefore, they do not get it; but those who are willing to obey shall have all the light they want.

It seems to me that we have come infinitely short of any right and rational idea of the aggressive spirit of the New Testament saints. Satan has gotten Christians to accept what I may call a namby-pamby, kid-gloved kind of system of presenting the Gospel to people. "Will they be so kind as to read this tract or book, or would they not like to hear this popular and eloquent preacher? They will be pleased with him quite apart from religion." That is the sort of half-frightened, timid way of putting the truth before unconverted people, and of talking to them about the salvation of their souls. It seems to me this is utterly antagonistic and repugnant to the spirit of the early saints: "Go ye and preach the Gospel to EVERY CREATURE," and again the same idea—"Unto whom now I send thee." Look what is implied in these commissions.

It seems to me that no people have ever yet fathomed the meaning of these two divine commissions. I believe the Salvation Army has come nearer to it than any people that have ever preceded them. Look at them. Would it ever occur to you that the language meant, "Go and build chapels and churches and invite the people to come in, and if they will not, let them alone." "GO YE." "If you sent your servant to do something for you, and said, "Go and accomplish that piece of business for me," you know what it would involve. You know that he must see certain persons, running about the city to certain offices and banks, and agents, involving a great deal of trouble and sacrifice; but you have nothing to do with that. He is *your servant.* He is employed by you to do that business, and you simply commission him to "go and do it."

What would you think if he went and took an office and sent out a number of circulars inviting your customers or clients to come and wait on his pleasure, and when they chose to come, just to put your business before them? No, you would say, "Ridiculous." Divesting our

minds of all conventionalities and tradition-
alisms, what would the language mean? "Go
ye!" "To whom?" "To every creature." "How am
I to get to them?" WHERE THEY ARE. "Every
creature." There is the extent of your commission. Seek them out; run after them, wherever
you find a creature that has a soul—there go
and preach my Gospel to him. If I understand it,
that is the meaning and the spirit of the commission.

And then again, to Paul, he says, "Unto
whom now I send thee, to open their eyes, *and* to
turn *them* from darkness to light, and *from* the
power of Satan unto God." They are asleep—go
and wake them up. They do not see their danger.
If they did, there would be no necessity for you
to run after them. They are *preoccupied.* Open
their eyes, and turn them around by your des-
perate earnestness and moral suasion and moral
force. And, oh, what a great deal one man can do
for another, it makes me tremble to think! "Turn
them from darkness to light, and from the power
of Satan unto God." How did Paul understand it?
He says, "We persuade men." Do not rest content with just putting it before them, giving them
gentle invitations, and then leaving them alone.
He ran after them, poor things, and pulled them
out of the fire.

Take the bandage off their eyes which Satan
has bound round them. Knock, hammer, and
burn in, with the fire of the Holy Ghost, your
words into their poor, hardened, darkened
hearts, until they begin to realize that they are

IN DANGER, that there is something amiss. Go after them. If I understand it, that is the spirit of the apostles and of the early Christians; for we read that when they were scattered by persecution, they "went *everywhere* preaching the Word." The laity, the new converts, the young babes in Christ. It does not mean always in set discourses, and public assemblies, but they went after men and women, like ancient Israel—"every man after his man," to try and win him for Christ.

Some people seem to think that the apostles laid the foundations of all the churches. They are quite mistaken. Churches sprang up where the apostles had never been. The apostles went to visit and organize them after they had sprung up, as the result of the work of the early laymen and women going everywhere and preaching the Word. Oh, may the Lord shower upon us in this day the same spirit!

We should build churches and chapels; we should invite the people to them; but do you think it is consistent with these two commissions, and with many others, that we should rest in this, when three parts of the population utterly ignore our invitations and take no notice whatever of our buildings and of our services? *They will not come to us.* That is an established fact. What is to be done? They have souls. You profess to believe that as much as I do, and that they must live forever. Where are they going? What is to be done? Jesus Christ says, "Go after them."

When all the civil methods have failed; when the genteel invitations have failed; when one man says that he has married a wife, and another that he has bought a yoke of oxen, and another that he has bought a piece of land— then does the Master of the feast say, "The ungrateful wretches, forget about all of them!"? "No!" (see Luke 14:21–24). He says, "Go out into the highways and hedges, and compel them to come in, that my house may be filled. I will have guests, and if you can't get them in by civil measures, use military measures. Go and COMPEL them to come in." It seems to me that we want more of this determined, aggressive spirit. Those of you who are right with God— you want more of this spirit to thrust the truth upon the attention of your fellowmen.

People say that you must be very careful, very judicious. You must not thrust religion down people's throats. Then, I say, you will never get it down. What! Am I to wait till an unconverted, godless man *wants* to be saved before I try to save him? He will never want to be saved till the death rattle is in his throat. What! Am I to let my unconverted friends and acquaintances drift down quietly to damnation, and never tell them about their souls, until they say, "If you please, I want you to preach to me!" Is this anything like the spirit of early Christianity? No. Verily we must *make* them look—tear the bandages off, open their eyes, make them bear it. And if they run away from you in one place, meet them in another, and let them have no peace until they submit to God and get their souls saved.

This is what Christianity *ought* to be doing in this land, and there are plenty of Christians to do it. Why, we might give the world such a time of it that they would get saved in very *self-defense* if we were only up and doing, and determined that they should have no peace in their sins. Where is our zeal for the Lord? We talk of Old Testament saints, but I would we were all like David. "Rivers of water ran down his eyes because men kept not the Law of his God." But you say, "We cannot all hold services." Perhaps not. Go as you like. Go as quietly and softly as the morning dew. Have meetings like the Friends, if you like, ONLY DO IT. Don't let your relatives and friends, and acquaintances die, and their blood be found on your skirts!

I shall never forget the agony depicted on the face of a young lady who once came to see me. My heart went out to her in pity. She told me her story. She said, "I had a proud, ungodly father, and the Lord converted me three years before his death, and, from the very day of my conversion, I felt I ought to talk to him, and plead, and pray with him about his soul, but I could not muster up courage. I kept intending to do it, and intending to do it, until he was taken ill. It was a sudden and serious illness. He lost his mind, and died unsaved." And she said, "I have never smiled since, and I think I never shall any more." Don't be like that. Do it quietly, if you like; privately, if you like; but do it.

And do it as if you felt the value of their souls, and as if you intended to save them, if by any possible means in your power it could be done.

I had been speaking in a town, in the West of England, on the subject of *responsibility* of Christians for the salvation of souls. The gentleman with whom I was staying had winced a bit under the truth, and instead of taking it to heart in love, and making it the means of drawing him nearer to God, and enabling him to serve Him better, he said, "I thought you were rather hard on us this morning." I said, "Did you? I should be very sorry to be harder on anybody than the Lord Jesus Christ would be."

He said, "You can push things to extremes, you know. You were talking about seeking souls, and making sacrifices. Now, you are aware that we build the chapels and churches, and pay the ministers, and if the people won't be saved, we can't help it." (I think he had given pretty largely to a chapel in the town.) I said, "It is very heartless and ungrateful of the people, I grant; but, my dear sir, you would not reason thus in any temporal matter. Suppose a plague were to break out in London, and suppose that the Board of Health were to meet and appropriate all the hospitals and public buildings they could get for the treatment of those diseased, and suppose they were to issue proclamations to say that whoever would come to these buildings should be treated free of charge and every care and kindness bestowed on them, and the treatment would certainly cure them.

"But, supposing the people were so blind to their own interests, so indifferent and hardened that they refused to come, and consequently, the plague was increasing and thousands dying, what would you in the provinces say? Would you say, 'Well, the Board of Health has done what it could, and if the people will not go to be healed, they deserve to perish; let them alone!' No, you would say, 'It is certainly very foolish and wicked of the people, but these men are in a superior position. They understand the matter. They know and are responsible for the consequences. What in the world are they going to do? Let the whole land be depopulated?' No! If the people will not come to them, they must go to the people, and force upon them the means of health, and insist that proper measures should be used for the suppression of the plague." It needed no application. He understood it, and I believe, by the Spirit of God, he was enabled to see his mistake, to take it home, and set to work to do something for perishing souls.

People are preoccupied, and it is for us to go and force it upon their attention. Remember, you can do it. There is some *one soul* that you have more influence with than any other person on earth—some soul, or souls. Are you doing all you can for their salvation? Your relatives, friends, and acquaintances *are* to be rescued. Thank God! we are rescuing the poor people all over the land by thousands. There they are, to be looked at, and talked with, and questioned—people rescued from the depths of sin, degradation, and woe—saved from the worst forms of crime and infamy; and, if He can do that, He can save your genteel friends, if only you will go to them desperately and determinedly. Take them lovingly by the button-hole, and say, "My dear friends, I never spoke to you closely, carefully, and prayerfully about your soul." Let them see the tears in your eyes; or, if you cannot weep, let them *hear the tears in your voice* and let them realize that you feel their danger, and are in distress for them. God will give His Holy Spirit, and they *will be saved.*

I was going to note that both texts imply opposition—for, He adds, "Lo, I am with you always, even unto the end of the world" (Matthew 28:20). As much as if He had said, "You will have need of my presence. Such aggressive, determined warfare as this will raise all earth and hell against you." And then He says to Paul, "I will be with thee, delivering thee from the people and the Gentiles unto whom I send thee." Why would they need this? Because the Gentiles would soon be up in arms against him, and indeed they were.

Opposition! It is a bad sign for the Christianity of this day that it provokes so little opposition. If there were no other evidence of its being wrong, I should know it from that. When the church and the world can jog along comfortably together, you may be sure there is something wrong. The world has not altered. Its spirit is exactly the same as it ever was, and if Christians were equally faithful and devoted to the Lord, and separated from the world, living so that their lives were a reproof to all ungodliness, the world would hate them as much as ever it did.

It is the *church* that has altered, *not* the world. You say, "We should be getting into endless turmoil." Yes! "I came not to bring peace on the earth, but a sword" (see Matthew 10:34). There would be uproar. Yes! And the Acts of the Apostles are full of stories of uproars. One uproar was so great that the Chief Captain had to get Paul over the shoulders of the people, lest he should have been torn in pieces. "What a commotion!" you say. Yes; and, bless God, if we had the like now we should have thousands of sinners saved.

"But," you say, "see what a very undignified position this would bring the Gospel into." That depends on what sort of dignity you mean. You say, "We should always be getting into collision with the powers that be, and with the world, and what very unpleasant consequences would result." Yes, dear friends, there always have been unpleasant consequences to the flesh, when people were following God and doing His will. "But," you say, "wouldn't it be inconsistent with the dignity of the Gospel?" It depends from what standpoint you look at it. It depends upon what really constitutes the dignity of the Gospel.

What does constitute the dignity of the Gospel? Is it human dignity, or is it divine? Is it earthly, or is it heavenly dignity? It was a very undignified thing, looked at humanly, to die on the cross between two thieves. That was the most undignified thing ever done in this world, and yet, looked at on moral and spiritual grounds, it was the grandest spectacle that ever earth or heaven gazed upon, that the inhabitants of heaven gazed upon. And I think that the inhabitants of heaven stood still and looked over the battlements at that glorious, illustrious Sufferer, as He hung there between heaven and earth.

The Pharisees, I know, spat upon the humbled Sufferer, and wagged their heads and said, "He saved others, himself He cannot save." Ah! But He was intent on saving others. That was the dignity of Almighty strength allying itself with human weakness, in order to raise it. It was the dignity of eternal wisdom shrouding itself in human ignorance, in order to enlighten it. It was the dignity of everlasting, unquenchable love, baring its bosom to suffer in the stead of its rebellious creature—man. Ah! It was incarnate God standing in the place of condemned, apostate man—the dignity of love! *love!* LOVE!

Oh, precious Savior! Save us from maligning Thy Gospel and Thy name by clothing it with our paltry notions of earthly dignity, and forgetting the dignity which crowned Thy sacred brow as Thou didst hang upon the cross! That is the dignity for us, and it will never suffer by any gentleman here carrying the Gospel into the back slums or alleys of any town or city in which he lives. That dignity will never suffer by any employer talking lovingly to his servant maid or errand boy, and looking into his eyes with tears of sympathy and love, and trying to bring his soul to Jesus.

That dignity will never suffer, even though you should have to be dragged through the streets with a howling mob at your heels, like Jesus Christ, if you have gone into those streets for the souls of your fellowmen and the glory of God. Though you should be tied to a stake, as were the martyrs of old, and surrounded by laughing and taunting friends and their howling followers—that will be a dignity which shall be crowned in heaven, crowned with everlasting glory. If I understand it, *that* is the dignity of the Gospel—the dignity of love. I do not envy, I do not covet any other. I desire no other—God is my witness—than the dignity of love.

Oh, friends! Will you get this baptism of love! Then you will, like the apostles, be willing to push your limbs into a basket, and be let down by the wall, if need be, or suffer shipwreck, hunger, peril, nakedness, fire, or sword, or even go to the block itself, if thereby you may extend His kingdom and win souls for whom He shed His blood. The Lord fill us with this love and baptize us with this fire. And then the Gospel will arise and become glorious in the earth, and men will believe in us, and in it. They will feel its power, and they will go down under it by thousands, and by the grace of God, they SHALL.

2

The World's Need

"Son, go work today in my vineyard."
—Matthew 21:28

"And the Lord said unto the servant, Go out
into the highways and hedges, and compel
them to come in, that my house may be filled."
— Luke 14:23

We might have mentioned other texts
teaching the same truth. There are plenty of
them, but the general tenor and bearing of the
Word of God, especially of the New
Testament, is clear. It seems to me that no one
can disinterestedly and dispassionately study
the New Testament without arriving at the
conclusion that there is a fundamental principle underlying the whole. His light and grace
is expansive, teaching us that God has, in no
case, given His light, His truth, and His grace
to any individual soul, without holding that
soul responsible for communicating that light
and grace to others.

Real Christianity is, in its very nature and
essence, aggressive. We get this principle fully

exhibited and illustrated in the parables of Jesus Christ. If you will study them, you will find that He has not given us anything to be used merely for ourselves, but that we hold and possess every talent which He has committed to us for the good of others, and for the salvation of the lost. If I understand it, I say this is a fundamental principle of the New Testament.

How wonderfully this principle was exhibited in the lives of the apostles and early Christians! How utterly careless they seemed to be of everything compared with evangelism—this was the first thing with them everywhere! How Paul, at the very threshold, counted nothing else of any consequence, but willingly, cheerfully gave up every other consideration to live for this; and how he speaks of other apostles and helpers in the Gospel who had been nigh unto death, and laid down their necks for the work's sake; and we know how he traveled, worked, prayed, wept, and suffered, bled and died, for this one end.

Also the early Christians, scattered through the persecution, went everywhere preaching the Word. How earnest and zealous they were. Even after the apostolic age, we learn from ecclesiastical history, they would push themselves in everywhere, winning converts, and real, self-denying followers even in kings' courts. They would not be kept out, and could not be put down, and could not be hindered or silenced. "These Christians are everywhere," said one of their bitterest persecutors. Yes, they were instant in season and out of season. They won men and women on every hand, to the vexation and annoyance of those who hated them. Like their Master, they could not be hid; they could not be repressed, so aggressive, so constraining was the spirit which inspired and urged them on.

It becomes a greater puzzle every day to me, coming in contact with individual souls, how people read their Bibles! They do not seem to understand what they read. Well might a Philip or an angel come to them and say, "Understandest thou what thou readest?" Oh, friends, study your New Testament on this question, and you will be alarmed to find to what an awful extent you are your brother's keeper—to what an awful and alarming extent God holds you responsible for the salvation of those around you.

I want to glance, FIRST, at our *call to work for God;* and SECOND, at *two or three indispensable qualifications for successful labor.*

And, *first,* as I have just said, we are called by the Word not only in these direct passages, but by the underlying *principle* running through it all, and laying upon us the *obligation to save the lost.* In fact, the world is cast upon us; we are the *only people who* CAN *save the unconverted.* Oh, I wish I could get this thought thoroughly into your minds. It has been, perhaps, one of the most potent, with respect to any little service I have rendered in the vineyard—the thought that Jesus Christ has nobody else to represent Him here but we Christians. Nobody else to work for Him. These poor people of the world, who are in darkness and ignorance, have nobody else to show them the way of mercy. If we do not, by the power of the Holy Spirit, bind the strong man and take his goods, who is to do it? God has delegated it to us. I say this is an alarming and awful consideration.

Second, we are called by the Spirit. The very first aspiration of a newly born soul is to go after some other soul. The very first utterance, after the first burst of praise to God for deliverance from the bondage of sin and death, is a prayer gasped to the throne for some other soul still in darkness. And is not this the legitimate fruit of the Spirit? Is not this what we should expect? I take any one here, who has been truly saved, to record if the first gushings of his soul, after his own deliverance, were not for somebody else—father, mother, child, brother, sister, friend?

Oh, yes, some of you could not go to sleep until you had written to a distant relative, and poured out your soul in anxious longings for his salvation; you could not take your necessary food until you had spoken or written to somebody in whose soul you were deeply interested. The Spirit began at once to urge you to seek for souls; and so it is frequently the last cry of the Spirit in the believer's soul before it leaves the body.

You have sat beside many a dying saint, and what has been the last prayer? Has it been anything about self, money, family, circumstances? Oh, those things are now all left behind, and the last expressed anxiety has been for some prodigal soul outside the kingdom of God.

When the light of eternity comes streaming upon the soul, and its eyes get wide open to the value of souls, it neither hears nor sees anything else! It goes out of time into eternity, praying, as the Redeemer did, for the souls it is leaving behind. This is the first and *last utterance* of the Spirit in the believer's soul on earth. Oh, if Christians were only true to the promptings of this blessed Spirit, it would be the prevailing impulse, the first desire and effort all the way through life. It is not God's fault that it is not so.

In personal dealing with souls, no point comes out more frequently than this: nothing which those who have really been converted and become backsliders in heart more frequently confess and bemoan than their unfaithfulness to the urgings of the Spirit with respect to other souls. In fact, backsliding begins here in thousands of instances. Satan gets people to yield to considerations of ease, propriety, being out of season, being injudicious, and so on, and they lose opportunities of dealing with souls, and so the Spirit is grieved and grieved. Oh, what numbers of people have confessed this to me.

A gentleman, in advanced life, said: "When I was a young man, and in my first love, the zeal of the Lord's house so consumed me that I used to neglect my daily business, and could scarcely sleep at night. But alas, that was many years ago." "Was it not better with you then than now?" I asked; and the tears came welling up into his eyes. Oh, yes, the Lord says of him, "I remember thee, the kindness of thy youth, the love of thine espousals, when thou wentest after me in the wilderness, in a land that was not sown: Israel was holiness unto the Lord, and the firstfruits of His increase." (Jeremiah 2:2–3). And, alas, there are many such today. They have it all to do over again. They have to repent and do their first works. They have to come back and get forgiven, and washed, and saved, if they are to go into the kingdom on high, all for lack of systematically and resolutely obeying the urgings of the Holy Spirit toward their fellowmen.

Now, some of you have been hearing about grieving the Spirit, and about being filled with the Spirit; and some of you are puzzled as to how you ought to wait—whether you ought to go on with your lawful avocations and wait. I say, my friends, this is the great point—you must so wait, wherever it may be; so plead and wrestle, and believe, THAT YOU GET IT. Then I care not whether it be in Jerusalem, in the Upper Room, or anywhere else—only, get it.

Don't let us lose the substance in quibbling about the way. Wait in the way congenial to your present circumstances; but, oh, wait for it until you get it, for this is the life of your souls, and the life of many souls, perchance, besides yours. You want this Spirit—the Spirit that yearns over the souls of your fellowmen; to weep over them as you look at them in their sin, and folly, and misery; the Spirit that cannot be satisfied with your own enjoyments or with feeling that YOU are safe, or even that your children are safe; but that yearns over every living soul while there is one left unsaved, and can never rest satisfied until it is brought into the kingdom.

Such are the urgings of the Spirit; and if people would only be obedient to them, they would never lose these urgings. Why, what an anomaly it is! Does it look reasonable, or like God's dealings, that people should begin, like the old man felt when he was young, and instead of waxing stronger, and having this holy zeal and desire increased, get weaker and weaker, and less and less? Does it look like God's way of doing things? Oh, no! This eclipse is through grieving and quenching the Spirit.

Now, my friend, you are called by the Spirit to this work. Obey the call—DO IT. Never mind if it chokes you—do it. Say, "I would rather die in obedience than lie in disobedience." Oh, these everlasting likes and dislikes. "I cannot speak to that person." "I cannot write that letter." "Oh, you don't know what would be the consequences." Never mind the consequences—do it. God will stand between you and the consequences; and, if He lets you suffer, never mind—then suffer; but obey the voice of the Spirit.

There would have been thousands of souls saved if all those who have had these urgings had obeyed them. Where do these urgings come from? Do they come from your own evil hearts? Then you are better than the apostle. Separated from the Spirit that dwells in you, and disunited from Christ, your living Head, you are selfish, *devilish*. Then where do these urgings come from? Do they come from the devil? Satan, then, would indeed be divided against himself. Where do they come from? It is the Spirit of the living God that is urging you to come out and seek to save the lost.

Will you obey these urgings? Will you give up your reasonings? Will you give up your likes and dislikes and OBEY? If you will, then He will come to you more and more, till, like David, you will feel the interests of His kingdom to be more to you than meat or drink, than silver or gold. Nay, you will become like him who said, "The zeal of Thine house hath eaten me up" (Psalm 69:9).

But, further, *we are called to this work by what He has done for us.* And what is that? Oh, you say, I cannot tell. No, no; we shall have to get *to heaven* first, and then we shall never be able to tell. We shall never be able to cast up that sum, not even for the gratification of the angels. That will remain an unexplored quantity forever, what He has done for us! We shall have to find out what it would have been to have been lost, and what it is to be saved in all its fullness and eternity, before we can tell what He has done for us!

What has He done for us? Oh, if we had a tithe of the love to sinners that He had for us, of His forbearing patience, of His persevering effort, when He followed us day and night, reasoned and reasoned with us, wooed and allured us, what could we not do?

I remember reading, somewhere, the story of a nobleman (Count Zinzendorf) who was, I think, a backslider. He was stopping at some country inn, and he went up into a room in which, over the mantelpiece, there was a very good picture of the crucifixion by a good old master, and under it was written, "I suffered this for thee—what hast thou done for me?" This question went home. It struck deep. He thought, "Yes, what indeed?" He went out into the stables to his horses, to try to get rid of the uncomfortable impression, but he could not forget it. A soft, pathetic voice seemed to follow him, "I suffered this for thee—what hast thou done for me?" At last it broke him down, and he went to his knees. He said, "True, Lord, I have never done anything for Thee, but now I give myself and my all to Thee, to be used in Thy service."

And have you never heard that voice in your soul, as you have been kneeling at the cross? Did you ever gaze upon that illustrious Sufferer, and hear His voice, as you looked back into the paltry past? "What hast Thou done for me?"

Now, there have been, at least, something like 350 people, who have come forward so far in these services, professing to give themselves afresh and fully to Jesus. I am sure, in the main, they have been sincere. They have come for the witness of the Spirit to their adoption, and for power for service. Now, friends, I want to know what this is to come to—what is to be the end of it?

> "What are you going to do, brother?
> What are you going to do?"

And, sister, too. Is it going to die out in sentiment? Is it going to evaporate in sighs and wishings, and end in "I CANNOT"? God forbid!

What are you GOING TO DO? What HAVE you been doing for Him the last week? Ask yourselves. You say, "Well, I have read my Bible more." Very good, so far as it goes. What have you read it for? "Well," you say, "to get to know the Lord's will and to get instruction and comfort." Aye, exactly, but that is all for *yourself,* you see. "I have prayed a great deal." Very good. I wish everybody would pray. The apostles say all men everywhere ought to pray. "I have been asking the Lord for great things." Very good, praise the Lord; but those are for yourself, mainly. If you have been led out in agonizing supplication for souls, thank God for it, and go on, and, as the apostle says, "Labour thereunto, with all perseverance, praying in the

Holy Spirit." But if it has been merely to get all you can for yourself, what profit is that to the Lord?

But you say, "l am bringing up my family." Exactly; so are the worldly people around you, but what for? For God or for yourself? Oh, let us look at these things, friends. I am afraid a great deal of religion is a mere transition of the selfishness of the human heart from the world to religion. I am afraid a great deal of the religion of this day ends in getting all you can and doing as little as you can—like some of your employees. You know the sort, who will do no more than they are forced—just get through, because they are hired. There is a great deal of that kind of service in these days, both toward man and toward God!

Now, friends, what have you been doing for Him—for the promotion of HIS blessed, glorious, saving purposes in the world? What have you been denying yourself for the sake of His kingdom? What labor have you gone through of mind, or heart? How many letters have you written? How many people have you spoken to? How many visits have you made? What self-denying labor have you been doing for Him who has done (as you say) so much for you? What have you been suffering for Him? Have you been trying to do some little measure "for His body's sake, the church" (see Colossians 1:24)?

Have you been carrying the sins and sorrows of the guilty world on your heart before

God and pleading with Him for His own Name's sake, to pour out His Spirit upon the ungodly multitudes outside, and to quicken half-asleep professors inside? Have you been subjecting yourself to reproach and contempt—not only from the world, but from half-hearted professors and Pharisees, bearing the cross, enduring the shame of unkind reproaches in living and striving to save them? Oh, what have you been doing, brother and sister?

Come now, friends, I want a practical result. He suffered that for you. He is in heaven interceding for you. Five bleeding wounds He always bears in the presence of His Father, for you. If He were to forget you for a single moment, or cease His intercession, what would happen? What are you doing for Him? He has left you an example that you should follow in His steps. What were they? They were blood-tracked; they were humble steps. They were steps scorned by the world. He was ignored and rejected of men. He had nowhere to lay His head. He carried in His body and in His soul the sorrows and sufferings of all people.

He was a man of sorrows—not His own. He had no reason to be sorrowful. He was the Father's own beloved, and He knew it, but He was a man of sorrows, and acquainted with grief. The griefs of this poor, lost, half-damned world He bore, and they were sometimes so intolerable that they squeezed the blood through His veins. Have you been following in His footsteps, in any measure? He lived not for Himself. He came not to be ministered unto, but to minister, and took upon Him the form of a servant. What are you doing? Oh, my friends, up, up, and be doing. Begin! If you have not begun—begin today. Ask Him to baptize you with His Spirit, and let you begin at once to follow Him in the regeneration of the Spirit. You are called by what He did for you!

Then, you are called by the needs of the world. I have said so much about this at other times that I will not say more now, only I think this is a theme that is never exhausted, and never will be while there are any more sinners to save. Oh, the needs of the world! To me it is an overwhelming, a prodigious thought, that He shed His blood for every soul, and that as He hung there, He saw, under all the vileness, and sin, and ruin of the Fall—the human soul created originally in His own image, and capable of infinite and eternal development and progress. The soul to be rescued, washed, redeemed, saved, sanctified, and glorified—He saw this glorious jewel and He gave HIMSELF for it.

Look at these souls. There is not one of them so mean, or vile, or base, but can be rescued by the power of His Spirit, and by His living, glorious Gospel brought to bear upon them. The Savior, quoting from the Prophets, says, "Ye are gods (and adds) the Scriptures cannot be broken" (see John 10:34,35). He had no such little, mean, insignificant estimate of the worth of human souls as some people have nowadays, who consign whole generations to hell without any bowels of mercy or compassion. Oh, the Lord fill us with the pity of Jesus Christ, who, when He saw the multitudes, wept over them.

Oh, friends, think of one such soul! What is your gold, or houses, or lands—what your respectability, what your reputation, what all the prizes of this world? We talk about it, but who realizes it—who, WHO?—the value of one precious, immortal soul, saved, redeemed, sanctified. Oh, the needs of the worldl They are dying, THEY ARE DYING! When people come to me with their fastidious objections, I say, "My friend, all I know is—souls are dying, dying."

If your homes were being decimated by the cholera, you would not be very particular about the means you used to stop it, and if anybody came with objections to the roughness of your methods, you would say, "The people are dying, they are dying," and that would be the end of all argument. I say, they are dying and they ARE TO BE SAVED. Satan is getting them: I want God to have them. Jesus Christ has bought them. He was the propitiation for the sins of the whole world. They belong to Him, and He shall have everyone I can reach, and everyone I can inspire others to reach also.

The world is dying. Do you believe it? You are called by the needs of the world. Begin nearest home if you like, by all means: I have little faith in those people's ministrations who go abroad after others, while their own are perishing at their firesides. Begin at home but do not end there. "Oh, yes," people say, "begin at home," but they end there. You never hear of them anywhere else, and it comes to very little, what they do at home, after all. God has ordained that the two shall go together. Get them saved by all means, but somebody else saved as well.

Set yourself to work for God. Go to Him to ask Him how to do it. Go to Him for the equipment of power, and then begin. Never mind how you tremble. I dare say your trembling will do more good than if you were ever so brave. Never mind the tears. I wish Christians would WEEP the Gospel into people. It would often go deeper than it does. Never mind if you do stammer. They will believe you when it comes from the heart. They will say, "He talked to me very naturally," as a man said, some time ago—wondering that he should be talked to about religion in a natural way. But be careful, no mock feeling, for they will detect it in a minute—yes, "be careful." Go off and pray until you get filled with the Spirit, and then go and let Him work through you. Finney says, "I went and let my heart out on the people."

Get your heart full of the living water and then open the gates and let it flow out. Look them in the face and take hold of them lovingly by the hand and say, "My friend, you are going to everlasting death. If nobody has ever told you till now—I have come to tell you. My friend, you have a precious soul. Is it saved?" They can understand that! Do not begin in a roundabout way, but talk to them straight, "Do you ever think about your precious soul? Are your sins pardoned? Are you ready to die?" Your neighbors, rich and poor, can understand that.

A lady said to my daughter, "I have begun talking to people about their souls in quite a different way to what I used to. I begin asking them if they do not know they are sinners and if they are ready to die, and it produces quite a different effect." For one reason, she has her own heart full of the love and Spirit of God, and that burns her words in. Begin in that way and see what God will do through you; for, of course, I only recognize you as the instrumentality which He has chosen, and those who reflect upon the instrumentality, reflect upon His wisdom. You go and put your hand to the plough and He will give you strength to push it along.

The Lord help you to go home thinking about the lost souls of the world.

Notes

Notes

Notes

Notes

Notes

Notes

Notes

Notes

Notes

Notes

Notes

Notes

Notes

Notes

Notes

Notes